THE LAWS OF CANUTE II THE GREAT

THE LAWS OF CANUTE II THE GREAT

SVEN AGGESEN

Copyright 2025 by Dalcassian Press

All rights reserved. No part of this book may be reproduced in any manner whatsoever without written permission except in the case of brief quotations embodied in critical articles and reviews.

No part of this publication may be reproduced, distributed, or transmitted in any form or by any means, including photocopying, recording, or other electronic or mechanical methods, without the prior written permission of the publisher, except in the case of brief quotations embodied in critical reviews and certain other non-commercial uses permitted by copyright law. For permission request, write to Dalcassian Press at admin@thescriptoriumproject.com

Translator: Curtin, D.P. (1985-)

ISBN: 979-8-3492-1617-6 (Paperback)
ISBN: 979-8-3492-1618-3 (Ebook)
Library of Congress Control Number:

Printed by Ingram Content Group, 1 Ingram Blvd, La Vergne, Tennessee
First Printing 2025, Dalcassian Press, Wilmington, DE

This work is part of series produced in association with the Scriptorium Project and its community of scholars and translators.
Please visit our website at: www.thescriptoriumproject.com

CANUTE II THE GREAT, KING OF DENMARK & ENGLAND

Laws of the military or court collected by Sven, son of Agen, grandson of Christiern.

PROLOGUE.

Since antiquity has left us many curious investigations, it also sought to provide for the utility of military society, lest the unrestrained youth of the army, having obtained wandering freedom, should impudently provoke each other with mutual insults without punishment. Hence, the most powerful kings of Denmark, to restrain the audacity of the wicked, decreed that a law should be promulgated from ancient memory, which they called Witherlogh in their own language, but we may refer to it in Latin, albeit with a less proper term, as the military or court law. Indeed, the antiquity of this law would have completely faded over time, as there have been very few to this day who have committed the affairs of past centuries, however illustrious, to memory and letters, unless the illustrious and greatest archbishop of the whole Danish kingdom, Absalon, with his usual curiosity, and careful and prudent deliberation with his foster father, King Canute, son of Waldemar, the first King of Denmark, had collected and instituted it into a small volume, as if into a register. For what is often deemed obsolete by antiquity is restored by the benefit of letters. Therefore, when I had found such constitutions written in our vernacular and indeed in succinct brevity, I endeavored to translate them into Latin, not truly with confidence in knowledge or talent, nor to make a presumption of arrogance that would prejudice those endowed with greater learning, but rather to provide a broader material for expression to be elaborated in a more elegant style. First, therefore, I shall speak of the founders of military laws; then, I will explain why and where these laws were promulgated.

CHAPTER I: ON CANUTE THE GREAT, FOUNDER OF THE MILITARY OR COURT LAWS.

King Canute, son of Sweno Tyugescheg, King of Denmark, having seized the ancestral kingdoms and provinces, magnificently expanded the boundaries of his dominion from the farthest Thule to the empire of the Greeks with an unconquerable strength. For, with power of vast magnitude almost equal to that of Alexander the Great, he reached England, Knut reduced Norway, Sclavonia, Finland, and all the surrounding regions to his power and subjected them to his native kingdom. Hence it happened that to his court, men of war flocked from all sides, who, because of the fame of his virtue and victory, eagerly and unhesitatingly dedicated themselves to the service of such a great prince. Therefore, a numerous crowd of military men gathered at his royal court; yet all did not excel in equal virtue.

CHAPTER II: ON THE REASON FOR THE ELECTION.

Wherefore King Knut finally directed his mind to this concern, to segregate the cohort of soldiers, previously in a somewhat confused order not differing from one another, according to the quality of their merits and the experience of their virtues. Moreover, he resolved to add to his own household those whom he had learned either to flourish by the titles of their lineage or to abound in the wealth of their resources, so that indeed those of noble descent might attain the height of virtue, and those raised in wealthier families would not be affected by poverty in their armament. Therefore, the herald announced that he ordered to be proclaimed that only those would experience the king's clemency and enjoy the privilege of closer familiarity above others, who would shine in the honor of the king and the dignity of the military cohort with their double-headed axes and golden-tipped swords. For it is fitting for the honor of the prince if the military assembly accompanies him, distinguished by shining arms, from all sides. After this edict was proclaimed, those whom poverty in their household pressed decided to separate themselves from the wealthier phalanx and to distinguish themselves as if completely alien. There was no delay: with the workshops of craftsmen resounding, all the cities echoed. Indeed, all the adornments, previously conspicuous in gold, were melted down by the work of goldsmiths, so that what had previously been gathered for vain uses of military pride might be transformed into exquisite axes and beautiful sword tips by the ingenuity of the goldsmiths. From this, it happened that (as the human mind is often inclined to ambition) each of the soldiers, sparing no expense, tried to surpass his fellow soldier in the splendor and craftsmanship of arms. Hence, it is clear that only those of elegant arms were deemed worthy of adornment, who were born and raised under more prosperous fortunes. When, however, according to the standard of the royal edict, a numerous phalanx, shining with a new kind of armament, had flowed into the court of Knut, it was decided that the entire multitude should be counted by a certain calculation number. The total amounted to three thousand selected soldiers. This cohort was decided to be called Thinglith in their own language.

CHAPTER III: ON THE REASON FOR THE INSTITUTION.

Therefore, since King Canute had united such discordant customs of nations into one family, it was necessary that the army of such a great king, being gathered from various nations, namely from all the kingdoms subdued to his dominion, whose manners, however, differed with immense variety, should be compelled to adhere to a uniform standard of military discipline. For nothing is more fitting for honorable comrades than that, all controversy being quelled, they serve one lord, not contending with each other, but with a common desire, and with no stain of discord, malice, or envy existing among them, united by a harmonious will, as the members of one body and like faithful followers, nurturing no sinister suspicion between themselves, they should unanimously obey the commands of one king.

Moreover, in order that King Canute might more rigorously constrain the looseness of military customs, he deemed it better to use severity against unruly and hot-headed recruits rather than excessive favor and lavish indulgence. For it would not have been easy to recall such a numerous following, very dissimilar in speech, manners, and character, to mutual concord, unless the severity of punishment tempered the precipice of excess and the magnitude of correction restrained the audacity of wrongdoing.

CHAPTER IV: ON THE CONDITION AND PLACE OF LAWS.

Therefore, when in England, having gathered his entire army, King Canute refreshed his weary limbs with the tranquility of rest after military labors, he summoned wise men to himself, particularly those whom he knew to be distinguished by their prudence, namely Opone of Zealand, nicknamed the Wise, and Eskil, his son, with whom he was accustomed to communicate and entrust the secrets of his counsel due to their experience in many matters (whom he had also appointed as his secretaries). With them, he engaged in serious deliberation on how to curb youthful insolence with strictness of discipline and to establish firm peace and concord among the soldiers for the future. Therefore, at their urging and counsel, he promulgated military laws, the fear of which would prevent anyone from daring to harm another in any way. And because human nature is prone to the precipice of transgression, it was necessary that precise remedies be applied to each case of wrongdoing. Consequently, he decided that both minor and serious offenses should be dealt with through careful measures. Thus, in order to expedite matters, let us pass over the more difficult matters and first examine the minutiae. For indeed, the cleverness of antiquity has labored with great effort to eliminate every scruple of controversy from the court of princes, so that not even the slightest cause for litigation might arise among the comrades, but rather that a certain bond of brotherly affection might unite their minds, which were burning with the desire to fight.

CHAPTER V: ON THE LAWS CONCERNING MINOR OFFENSES.

However, there was a custom among the ancient courtiers, who are still considered soldiers by name, that they would render alternate services to each other without their attendants and servants, and in turn serve one another. Hence, they established that if one of their comrades were to water his horse with his own, the other would ride when going and would lead when returning. But if someone, while being led on a borrowed horse to water, were to go and return while being drawn by the reins, and if he were convicted of the same offense three times by the testimony of two comrades, it was decided that he should remain outside while dining with one man. For it was customary that either according to the title of virtue, or the priority of time, or the lineage of nobility, soldiers would reside in assigned places, so that thus those of greater dignity or earlier time might occupy more worthy places. Hence, it is clear that no one could be removed from his usual place without singular insult and disgrace. They decreed that the same sentence would apply to one who, while grazing, extended his reins to his own horse but took straw from another, and on this, he should also be convicted by the testimony of two, as before. Likewise, if anyone, while watering horses against the current of a river, stirred up the water so that others could not drink from it unless it were turbulent, and it was established by similar testimony that he had done the same three times, he would be subject to similar judgment. For the same guilt is condemned by equal punishment. Furthermore, if someone noted an unyielding presumption with three offenses of disobedience and refused to repent, they decided to place him last of all. Indeed, they decreed that anyone convicted could throw bones at him at their discretion, nor would anyone be accused for this of rashness or insolence. Moreover, he should be content with his own dish and cup, with no one sharing in his drink and food. But indeed, if anyone's stubbornness were to want the king's clemency to protect him so much that he would be placed in the first seat as a collateral, they believed this indulgence should be granted to him by the prince, with the added condition that he be excluded from any assistance of comrades and exempted from the obligation of prior law.

CHAPTER VI: ON THE MUTUAL EXHIBITION OF FAVOR AND PAYMENT OF SALARIES.

But since the law was to be established for many matters, King Canute deemed it appropriate to begin from his principal dignity. Indeed, he wished to accommodate himself to the soldiers' discretion with a temperance of clemency and gentleness, in such a way that he himself would prescribe the form and necessity of obedience to them. Therefore, it was agreed that the king or any prince who wished to boast of the company of an army should, in turn, provide the loyalty he demands from his men, should display a cheerful countenance, and should not deny the grace of companionship and affability. He also deemed it worthwhile to establish that the king or prince should supply his soldiers with wages whenever necessity or need required, without delay and with all contradiction removed, so that they, having received their wages, would be entirely faithful, returning the kindness to their lords and being ready to comply with their commands and not neglecting to obey their orders. For it is in vain that one demands what he does not provide.

CHAPTER VII: ON THE RESIGNATION OF MINISTRY.

Ancient custom also did not neglect to establish a form whereby both the majesty of the prince would remain intact and the honor of the soldier would not be diminished if someone transferred his allegiance to another. Therefore, it was established that on the vigil of circumcision, which begins the new year, two comrades should be sent to the lord from the experienced soldier who desires to renounce his lordship, to resign his allegiance along with his service. Thus, without the shame of insult or the offense of the lord, anyone could freely transfer their allegiance to another.

CHAPTER VIII: ON INSULTS AND CONTUMELIES.

Moreover, since all wickedness tends to provoke strife and insults, it was also deemed appropriate to apply remedies to prevent comrades from inflicting mutual insults upon each other, interrupting the concord of fraternal union with discord, hatred, and spite. Therefore, the wisdom of antiquity considered that for such causes, a mature remedy of chastisement should be applied, so that the beginnings of quarrels and insults would be addressed. The authority of the law should be anticipated to be quelled in its very principles, before it could grow through prolonged delays. For wounds must be cut away with iron, which have not felt the healing of remedies. Therefore, if anyone were to afflict his comrade with insults or affronts, or provoke him with any injuries whatsoever, it was decided that an action should be instituted in the presence of the king, with all comrades gathered, in the meeting that is called Huskarlesteffne. If the accuser can prove his comrade to be guilty of the injury inflicted upon him in Witherloghmanne by the testimony of two of his comrades, so that the witnesses do not refuse to confirm their testimony under oath on the sacred things, it has been established that the accused should be placed outside in the usual hall with one man. It has also been determined by general constitution that any controversy arising between these comrades should be addressed or resolved nowhere except in the already named meeting.

CHAPTER IX: OF GENERAL CONTROVERSY.

It has also been established by a general constitution that any controversy arising among comrades regarding lands, estates, and fields, or even concerning the plundering of dwellings, which is called "boran" in our language, should be discussed in the aforementioned assembly. Then, the one to whom the judgment of the comrades will assign the right of sale, having drawn lots with six others in his group, that is, a fjarth, must claim for himself the continuous possession of his territory and will defend the prescription assigned by law. However, lesser controversies between two comrades are to be resolved by the testimony of witnesses, namely by the old constitution of the neighbors, one being interior and the other exterior, with the accused present in the chamber. Although modern practices often decree a moderation of rigor and impose a term for the cause, even in the matter of the present article, if someone can defend himself with two comrades acquired from anywhere.

CHAPTER X: OF THE FIRST VIOLATION OF THE LAW.

After a short passage of time following the constitution of the law, the assailant of human blood, the rival of prosperity, the hater and most fervent pursuer of justice and equity, that crafty seducer of the progenitors, Satan, having attacked the principal dignity, attempted to persuade the king to commit the violation of the law, so that, with the head infected by poison, he might infuse the virus of his corruption into the other members. For the law's founder, the king namely Canute, while he was still enjoying peace in England, was seized by a fit of rage and killed a certain soldier of his, having drawn his sword. Hence, the entire phalanx, overwhelmed by excessive rage, did not hesitate to rush to arms with the legions converging everywhere. However, when it became known that the king's hand was responsible for this slaughter, they gathered together and anxiously scrutinized what action was needed. Indeed, they were torn by ambiguous opinions and wavered in their judgment, unsure whether the leader should be punished for the novelty of the crime or whether he should be granted clemency. For if the king were subjected to the given sentence, he would be exterminated like a headless and fugitive from the region. On the other hand, if royal reverence were indulged, it would provide an example of corruption and leniency for others to commit offenses. Ultimately, this opinion pleased the entire cohort, that the royal majesty should prostrate itself in the middle of the assembly and await either leniency or severity. After this was done, raising the king, they themselves granted forgiveness and grace for the offense, unanimously shouting that, henceforth, with all dispensation removed, the one guilty of such transgression should not at any future time expiate the enormity of such a crime with any satisfaction, but should either suffer a capital sentence or at least, with tempered severity, be cast out as an exile and fugitive from all military fellowship with the disgraceful name, that is, nithingsorth.

CHAPTER XI: ON WOUNDS AND INJURIES AND THEIR SATISFACTION.

After the king's magnificence had thus expiated the offense of his transgression, that constitution concerning such a slaughter being entirely punishable endured with steadfast firmness throughout the times of eight kings: under the rule, namely, of the ancient Canute, who was the founder of the law; also his son Canute, who was nicknamed Auster or Durus, although he did not succeed his father in the kingdom, but during the continuous time was like a coadjutor to his father governing the kingdom; likewise Magnus the Good; Sweyn, son of Estreth; Harald Hein; Canute, who was crowned with martyrdom in the church of Othoni; Olav, his brother; Eric the Good; and before the reign of the ninth king, namely Nicholas, it was not violated. Then indeed Christian, son of Sweyn, wounded Thukon Dokæ with a drawn sword, and he was the first to violate the military law after the satisfaction of King Canute. After this act, King Nicholas found himself in a perplexing situation. For he thought that this would be contrary to the safety of his kingdom and would appear as contrary to all those related to the matter as the more powerful of the kingdom, if he were to be expelled from the king's court with the disgraceful title, that is, nithingsorth, especially since two of his brothers were the most famous bishops of that time, namely Ascerus, the first archbishop of Lund, and Sweyn, the bishop of Vigberg, that his two brothers, Eskillus and Aggo, and their revered father, Sueno, son of Trugoti, who was regarded among the foremost nobles of the kingdom in his time. They, valuing the safety of their honor more than their wealth, decided it was better to pay a heavy fine for the committed offense than to risk their reputation. Therefore, diligently investigating, they consulted Bo, son of Hæthen, a Wandal, because he was of advanced age and had been a distinguished soldier under the old Kanut, who is known to have established these military laws, with the addition of other elders who were accustomed to commend the deeds of past times to memory. They inquired of them whether any similar offense was remembered in recent times that had nonetheless been rectified by satisfaction. While, after careful deliberation, they could recall no such offense, Bo the Wandal responded as follows: "Since until now such a matter has been defined less precisely by the taxation of our ancestors, it seems worthwhile to prescribe a certain measure of satisfaction for our descendants. Therefore, let a penalty be established for all successors, which may restrain the audacity of wrongdoing by fear of its severity." Thus, with the agreement of the entire court and the consent of King Nicholas, the decree of a new constitution was proclaimed, namely that whoever, with presumptuous audacity and temerity, violated the provisions of the preceding law, that is, with a 'withering blow,' by wounding his comrade in the future, should pay the king forty marks in place of satisfaction; then he, to whom the injury was inflicted, should be obliged to pay forty marks, in addition to the increase of his disgrace, the weight of two marks of gold, which in our language is commonly called 'gorsum'; and all comrades bound by the same law should pay forty marks as a composition. However, as time passed (as is always the case with human nature inclined towards evil), Aggo Thuer wounded Eskillus, son of Ebbon, in Warvvath during a quarrel, in the house of Guidon the stableman, under the protection of King Nicholas. Upon this act, the king, greatly incensed, decided to capture the aforementioned Aggo with the full willingness of all the comrades, despite Guidon's resistance and opposition. For he also offered the same measure of satisfaction that Christian had paid, as I mentioned above; which is said to have been done in Lynum at the hands of Bo, son of Ketilli. After this, as subsequent evils increased, satisfaction for the mentioned crime was thereafter instituted by the example of the first satisfaction and continued through long usage.

CHAPTER XII: ON STRIKING AND PERCUSSION.

However, if anyone should happen to strike a comrade, provoking him with a fist or any weapon, the rigor of the old constitution applies, provided that the act of two testimony of comrades has established that it admits no satisfaction whatsoever for expiation. However, the leniency of modern times has begun to mitigate this with a new temperance of the law. For if it has been established by such evident sign or testimony of fact that the accused can in no way defend himself against denial, it has been decided that he should fall at the feet of the one to whom he has brought shame, so that such a most disgraceful dishonor may be expiated by the humblest formula of satisfaction. But if the accuser has not been able to convict the accused with witnesses, it has been decreed by general constitution that he who makes the accusation should abolish his own infamy with six comrades.

CHAPTER XIII: ON VARIOUS CASES OF WOUNDS.

As the ancient serpent has various suggestions, the cases of those who are attacked are diverse. For it often happens that someone inflicts a wound on another either knowingly or unknowingly; likewise, the knowing one sometimes injures his own and sometimes another's; also, the ignorant one may injure either his own or another's. If someone knowingly and prudently wounds his comrade, he shall make satisfaction according to the prescribed form. But if he unknowingly and ignorantly inflicts a wound on his comrade, wishing to harm another, and by chance has injured him, he must defend and excuse his ignorance and the fact that he did it unwillingly with the testimony of three comrades; but if he fails in his defense, he shall settle with the injured party according to the aforementioned form of satisfaction. If, however, someone knowingly and prudently wounds his comrade, but is unaware that he is bound by the prescribed law, it has been decided that such ignorance does not excuse him from the guilt of transgression. For the same laws have been established to prevent anyone of military excellence from obscuring the flower of ignorance with the soot of negligence. Indeed, it is fitting to live honorably, and noble men of distinguished blood should not tarnish their noble titles through ignorance and laziness. Therefore, by general constitution, it has been determined that all controversies, which are divided by the decision of laws, should be settled by the sixth hand of comrades, as elders, or by the third or second, such as those of middle rank or minor, as we have explained above.

CHAPTER XIV: ON TREASON AND THE CRIME OF HIGH TREASON.

Having now enumerated the laws by which lesser controversies were decided in ancient times, it remains for us to address greater matters. When, however, the cunning enemy, the devil, daily seeks only to ensnare us with his deceptions, he cunningly makes us ascend from one excess to another, as if by steps, so that finally we may reach the destruction of condemnation, having completed the crimes. For when he has exercised his pestiferous suggestion on his satellites in small matters, he then incessantly invites them to a greater downfall. Thus, those whom he had previously taught to quarrel to the point of slaughter with their comrades, he finally attacks more boldly and incites them to not hesitate to plot death against their lord and prince through treachery. Therefore, if anyone has made himself guilty by detesting this deed, as one who has dared to contrive a plot of treachery against his lord, they have deemed him worthy of condemnation not only to loss of life but also of all his substance. Thus, they have decreed that there should be a gathering in this manner, if anyone has been accused of treachery or of the crime of majesty by the king. Until the wind has filled the sails in such a way that he has withdrawn himself from the sight of those watching; or if, with the Favonian wind not favoring, he has driven the waves with oars until he has withdrawn the sight of all the oars from their eyes, they are to be held waiting on the shore. But when they think they have advanced a little further into the sea to hide, they must resign the rights of the ancient confederation by calling out three times with the blast of the trumpet. But if he has appeared in his native land and incurred the crime of the aforementioned wickedness, the entire military company is bound to accompany him to the density of the woods and to wait at the edge of the grove until he has so retreated, selecting any dark cover, that he will not be able to hear their shout or call. Then the entire legion of comrades will strongly proclaim with three loud cries, so that no other way may be able to return to them.

Having done this, they are bound by this law, that if any comrade, with at least one companion or weapon, later encounters him and does not seize him, he must undergo the loss of the same disgrace and infamous designation. And thus far, as much as I could investigate through diligent inquiry from the ancients, I have pursued the military laws, although not in very polished language. It remains for our successors to supplement the deficiency of this adorned discourse and to complete this treatise in a more elegant style.

This work was produced in association with:

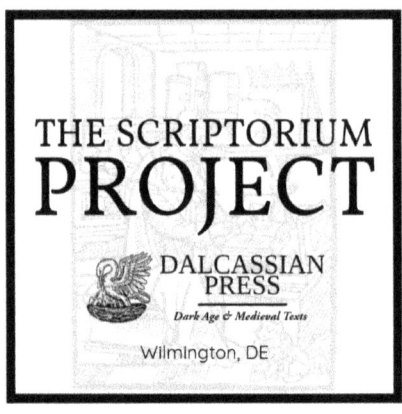